ORGANIZATIONAL CONUNDRUMS & PARADOXES (REVISED)

Leading Through the Gray Areas of Business

Dr. Indra Nath Chatterjee

BlueRoseONE.com
Stories Matter
NewDelhi • London

BLUEROSE PUBLISHERS
India | U.K.

For permissions requests or inquiries regarding this publication, please contact:

BLUEROSE PUBLISHERS
www.BlueRoseONE.com
info@bluerosepublishers.com
+91 8882 898 898
+4407342408967

ISBN: 978-93-7542-976-0

Cover design: Aafiya Saifi
Typesetting: Manisha Rawat

First Edition: December 2025

The Book is dedicated to my parents who inculcated basic values in me to become a good human being, and to some of my mentors who guided me during my professional journey.

PREFACE OF REVISED EDITION

After publication of previous version, I received a few suggestions from readers to elaborate on views expressed in some articles with examples in to make it more meaningful and enriching. I accepted those feedbacks with humility and gratitude and tried to work on the suggested line to bring out this expanded version. Hope readers may find it useful. I have also added an article 'Random Thoughts' based on my perceptions on contemporary landscape in this edition. Views are personal, broad based and holistic, and in no way intended to undermine brand equity of any organization or tarnish the image of any individual.

As mentioned earlier I am not an author per say except an attempt to bring out my learnings and observations during my professional years. Hope readers may find it useful and thought provoking.

PREFACE

I decided to articulate some of my own learnings in the form of few articles based on observations during my professional years in a few organizations. Objective is to share some thoughts for the benefit of the potential readers' particularly young aspiring management graduates embarking on a promising career. It will be my reward if a few readers find this brief articles useful. By stroke of any imagination, I do not claim myself an author or a management expert. My efforts through these monographs are to present brief contours of failures and paradoxes as seen during my professional years while bits of the contents derived from information available in public domain. Views expressed are personal and in no way intended to undermine brand equity of any organization or any individual. I purposely decided not to quote name of any organization and should be read more as a learning aid.

I am thankful to Dr. Subir Chowdhury, Former Director of Indian Institute of Management, Calcutta for going through my manuscript and gave valuable suggestions for enrichment of the content.

I am also thankful to Mr. V. Raghavan of Chennai for provoking me to write something on office politics sharing his own experiences.

While care has been taken to avoid misspelling or mistakes, I shall be obliged if any reader has any observation or views, please share the same to the author for guidance, learning, and for necessary corrective measures.

Book Summary:
(Organizatioanal Conundrum and Paradoxes (Rewvised)

The write ups highlight Author's own learnings and observations during his professional journey while working in different organizations at senior executive levels including board levels both in PSUs and Private Corporate sectors, in the form of a few articles on various management topics. Author has articulated his perceptions and insight in the areas of leadership, boss – subordinate relationships, organizational behavior in chaotic situation, dichotomy in budgetary exercise, pitfalls in organizational restructurings, conundrums in strategy implementation, causes of organizational decay, on corporate governance practices, office conflicts, etc. highlighting various paradoxes in management processes. The book also contains author's random thoughts on contemporary socioeconomic and geopolitical disruptive environment.

Views expressed are personal without undermining brand equity of any organization or any individual. It is hoped that the readers, practicing managers, management students, and others would find the articles enriching and thought provoking.

CONTENTS

1.
Leadership Revisited For Organizational Effectiveness

How good organizations over a period turned into ordinary or bad from a good phase and could not be able to sustain growth momentum? Why some companies make the leap and others don't? Is it leadership alone, 0r its operating culturc, core values, resource planning, nimbleness and agility to change with changes in the environment, market competitiveness, technology, customer preferences, or a balanced mix of all those factors based on balanced scorecard? While several management gurus have explored this area with a plethora of literatures and research reports ideating on concepts and thought processes ("Good to Great", "In Search of Excellence", "Built to Last", "Blue Ocean Strategy" and many more) but nothing suits each and every case as a right fit. Over time, lack of right kind of leadership, desired organizational changes, technology shift, or lack of innovative and entrepreneurial mindset made even a great organization mediocre and eventually lapsed into oblivion. Perhaps, continuous innovation and new learning are required to remain ahead of the pack.

In India, PSUs are much maligned corporate entities. Most of the PSUs suffer from hierarchical structure, often top heavy, frequent political and bureaucratic interventions, lack of succession planning for board level positions. The management continuity at the top level in PSUs often missed, since board level positions including that of CMDs are decided by the Govt. as owner, and often for shorter tenures. By the time, they start contributing they were superannuated or replaced by new persons, from within or outside. A person coming from outside as CMD or Director often comes with his or her baggage and some mandates from the Govt. It takes time for new person to understand the organizational ethos, culture and work style. Again each such top leader, brings his or her own style of leadership and tries to be judgmental Iin existing work culture which could be dysfunctional or disruptive. By the time, he creates his own acceptability and in the groove, he nears his superannuation period and new incumbent takes over.

Thus PSUs often suffer from frequent changes at the top hierarchy resulting disruptions in the organizations. Despite Govt.'s well-meaning intention of providing greater autonomy to PSUs depending upon the sector, scale, and size, at the implementation level, there is same 'business as usual' approach with political and bureaucratic interventions, diluting intended objectives. The hierarchical structure in PSUs also creates bottleneck in faster decision making slowing down efficient project management and implementations. PSUs are also saddled with excessive scrutiny of its activities by various external agencies, like, CAG, CVC, CBI, COPU, etc. having superior authority without much of accountability for results. Under such a setup, managers often act cautiously and avoid bold decisions and have a tendency to pass the buck to the higher levels despite availability of appropriate delegated powers. Thus in PSUs, top management or executive committee, most of the time, engaged in the matters which otherwise could have been decided at lower levels in accordance with delegated authority, power, and responsibility. Thus, quite often, top management gets bogged down with day to day activities instead of focusing its attention on big picture, risk management, and growth objectives.

Under such a situation, role of leadership becomes crucial. A leader who not only leads from the front but also manages astutely external environment through persuasive and rational argument to reduce impact of such external influence and protect the organization. A true leader builds up fellow leaders, not followers, who are capable of facing challenges and finding solutions for organization's greater good.

During my engagement in a large, premier PSU, I had come across such leadership disruptions and resultant consequences in the organization. During my initial years I came across the then Executive Chairman who had an exceptional leadership qualities and larger than life image. He was empathetic, had a sensitive approach to man management and dealings with people having uncanny knack of remembering names and faces. He used to manage the external environment with deft and fineness while jealously guarding the organization from external influences including bureaucracy. During his tenure brand equity of the organization grew many fold with international acclaim. With his leadership style and charismatic personality, he was like a big banyan tree under which many used to take shelter, but none grew up like him to lead the organization with same zest and vigor. Board level succession planning in most PSUs was rather limited as the same was in the hands of Public Executive Selection Board (PESB) and the Government through Cabinet Appointments Committee and selection was not always based on merit but on other considerations. On his departure, the organization lost one of best and longest serving Chairmen leaving behind his legacy of strong leadership, a well-known brand, and a growth strategy. Unfortunately, interim leadership and subsequent regular Chairmen so appointed at least for quite some time were not able to steer the organization to demonstrate the strong leadership and the vision needed at that stage. In fact, the next Chairman so appointed came from the IAS Cadre via the Chairmanship of the largest downstream company. His style of functioning created a gap between him and other executive board members who had to seek an appointment to meet the Chairman for any discussion forgetting the golden rule that the Chairman was one among equals for board level functioning and efficient corporate governance.

It is agreed that corner room occupant has to manage emerging situations in his own style so as to achieve results, but might not get best output without the support of other team members.

Before we deliberate on this further, let us look into leadership virtues as articulated by various management gurus and thought leaders. In fact, Harvard Business Review is full of thought provoking articles on leadership.

Daniel Goleman states leadership requires more of emotional intelligence (EI) than cognitive abilities. Emotional intelligence, according to him, covers self-awareness, self-regulation, motivation, empathy and social skills. Cognitive skills like big picture thinking and long-term vision are equally required. EI distinguishes outstanding leaders linked with strong performance. A natural leader's mettle is demonstrated and tested in adverse, disruptive and challenging situations. Most of corner room occupants fall prey to soft options during difficult times, like laying off employees or mass scale retrenchment, salary freeze, reduction in capital spending and other cost cutting measures including hiving off or closure of businesses, mergers, demergers, etc. All those measures did not call for any EI. Such actions often led to economic hardships not only on personnel so affected but on social economy with adverse multiplier effects. A true leader takes advantage of disruptive situation to prepare the organization for the future not always by such soft options but by identifying new avenues or blue ocean strategies for growth, not only retaining talents but by opportunistic new acquisitions by deploying surplus manpower as identified after reskilling and retraining. That's the challenge and proof of a great leader.

While there are a plethora of studies and articles on leadership by several authors and management gurus and thought leaders, it is observed going through some of them that there were a common thread running through most of such ideas except difference in perspectives, presentations and articulation.

Ronald A. Heifez and Donald L. Lawrie in their article talk about adaptive behavior of leaders when companies face adaptive challenges due to changes in societies, markets, customers, competition, technological shifts forcing organizations to clarify their values, develop new strategies, and adaptation to new ways of operations. Adaptive behavior challenges conventions resulting new perspectives, new strategies, new structures and operating culture to make the organization reinvent.

Warren J. Bennis and Robert J. Thomas viewed that leadership should possess four essential skills, 'the ability to engage others', 'a distinctive and compelling voice', 'a sense of integrity including a strong set of values', and 'an adaptive capacity'.

Jim Collins talked about Level 5 Leadership i.e. a leader who builds enduring greatness through a paradoxical combination of personal humility with intense professional will besides capabilities of other lower level as classified by him. From his research he had identified five levels of leadership hierarchy as under:

Level 1 – Highly capable individual who makes productive contribution through talent, knowledge, skills and good work habits.

Level 2 – Contributes to the achievements of group objectives, works effectively with others in a group setting.

Level 3 – Competent manager who organizes people and resources toward the effective and efficient pursuit of predetermined objectives.

Level 4 – Effective leader: catalyzes commitment to and vigorous pursuit of a clear and compelling vision, stimulates the group to high performance standards.

Level 5 – a leader having exceptional qualities of knowledge, skill, strong professional will, visionary combined with personal humility and empathetic approach as explained above.

Going by those leadership traits as outlined by Jim Collins, most of the organizations suffers from such quality of leadership needed in times of disruptions. It is true that a long term CEO has the opportunity to define the strategies and could make appropriate cultural and structural changes to implement the strategies. For example, Jack Welch, famed and most admired CEO of General Electric, held his position from 1981 till 2001, and transformed General Electric into a multiproduct, multinational organization as number one for a sustained period during his time through his aggressive style of leadership. However, some of his actions and unpopular decisions created lot of hardship and distress to large number of employees. He believed in doing things faster and better and set the bar higher for himself and for his team members and tolerated mistakes so long intentions were honest and were in the organization's interest. The tremendous financial achievements alongside his charismatic presence earned GE the Most Admired Company award by Fortune for four consecutive years. But there was a grey area which was hardly noticed, and that was accounting jugglery. As Serwer brought out that GE used accounting practices that obfuscated its true performance by using gains and losses from some businesses mainly financial services to offset gains and losses in other divisions. James Martin, a former GE employee in his book on Jack Welch has highlighted the questionable morality, the downsizing, the slippery and opaque accounting moves, the overwhelming pressure to make numbers and often shocking lack of respect for human dignity characterized his regime. Post retirement, Mr. Welch, somewhat fell from his grace due to receipt of one of largest severance payment in US corporate history at that time. Going by Jim Collin's categorization of leaders, author views that Jack Welch did not fit in Level 5 of leadership category as he lacked personal humility and empathy though he possessed strong professional will.

Thus many corner room occupants even of great organizations, going by various narratives, lack the quality needed to steer the organization to greatness and long-term sustainability missing growth opportunities.

According to Haskett, Emeritus Professor of Harvard Business School, Strategy is hard and Culture is soft. The impact of strategy on growth and profit can be measured, but that of a culture cannot. A strong culture which takes time for assimilation contributes to assured performances. According to his arguments, basic efforts to lead substantial change have to be completed in a reasonable time frame for desired results. He believed that change of culture is a continuous process and culture has to be linked with performance and profit though difficult to measure. For this, employee and customer engagement are needed bolstering innovation. To achieve that, leaders must take extra efforts to communicate their strategies, thought processes and approach across the organization through needed empowerment, belief, and trust for the teams.

A successful leader creates sustained growth and returns to stakeholders' on a long-term basis which makes the organization good to great. Leaders who are egoistic and self-seeker of personal glories often destroys the organization. On the other hand who create lasting values are remembered and respected. In their article about 'Authentic Leadership', Bill George, Peter Sims, Andrew N Mclean and Diana Mayer have stated the characteristics of authentic leaders as those who balance extrinsic and intrinsic motivation, practices values and principles and are grounded, create support teams and empowers people to lead.

While commenting on K Matsushita, the legendary Japanese owner of famed Matsushita Electrics, John P. Kotter used to believe that peace, prosperity and happiness would come from open-minded people with humanistic values. He combined the pragmatic with the spiritual, to hold on the earthly virtues and at the same time achieve phenomenal success in a fiercely competitive world. Most of Japanese Companies believed in people's power through cooperation, mutual respect and consensus against individualistic employees and that's why Japanese businesses are so successful.

Closer at home, Tata Groups philosophy is also more akin to Japanese people centric sense of values. J R D Tata the founder of Tata Group believed that profit and shareholders gain were not the sole motives and implemented the welfare of people both inside and outside the factory. Corporate social responsibility and corporate governance which are being talked about so much now a days, Tata had realized long ago the importance of not only shareholder value but also other stakeholder values.

Based on Author's personal experience, quite often, many not so deserving people got promoted to higher levels due to their proximity to the bosses and often proved to be misfits, more so during trying times, to the detriment of the organization, and the organization decays gradually. This tribe flourishes in most of the organizations be it in PSUs or in Private enterprises including multinationals. In this context author had come across several youngsters whose career got spoilt despite potential, due to whimsical attitude, racial prejudices, biases, unjust demands or expectations from higher ups. More particularly, if the organization is geographically spread out like many multinational companies or business conglomerates with unequal distribution of asset base, chances are that one would find many otherwise good talents are rotting at the same position or scale year after year without much of individual growth or motivation, being out of sight and out of mind of superiors. When a good suggestion voiced by a subordinate, such individual is ignored, snubbed or humiliated by seniors without appreciating such efforts on the part of talented youngsters, which could have provided strength to the seniors as well as to the organization.

Author had seen this attitude in many support service areas. The heads of such areas often lack leadership qualities and behaved more like parasites holding on to their chairs by keeping their bosses in good humor through various means which causes enormous damage to the organization. Unfortunately, in many organizations, such tribes thrive to the detriment of the organization. To allow such people to rise to the position of power and to the level of incompetence, would be disastrous for the organization. Author views that it is a failure on the part of HR as well as top leadership. Besides HR, it was the role of seniors and leadership to identify potential talents, bring them to the main stream after suitable training for greater good of the organization. A good talent always an asset and strengthened one's position instead of perceiving such junior as a threat to his or her position, hence to be ignored. A boss could gravitate to a leadership position when he or she recognizes importance of mentorship and grooming role with empathy. A good boss never confined to his or her room but walks around to subordinates offices to encourage and motivate his or her juniors.

Author had come across several categories of bosses during his professional years (a separate article on this topic follows) and found many of them were self-seekers, street smart and cunning. They expressed their loyalty to the bosses and often lacked commitment to the organization without much of professional ethics and quality of leadership needed. While the individual requires to be smart, intelligent and skillful in his understanding of organizational dynamics and should be able to manage interpersonal relationship, those attributes should not be at the cost of individual value judgment, loyalty to the organization and professional ethics.

Author's experience reflected that majority were followers and tended to follow existing practices of predecessors without much of inquisitiveness and mental applications like, what is the right way to go about, is there a better approach to manage things, etc. It's a question of organizational culture. A value based organization allows its employees to experiment and take risks. In the absence of such encouragement, the organization continued to remain mediocre and tends to decay. Only a handful did not straight away follow the conventions but analyze, interpret and search for alternatives for better outcomes. Such few employees show leadership traits and become main assets to the organization. As the saying goes organization is often run on eighty – twenty formula, which means while twenty percent contributes, eighty percent enjoys the privileges. It is up to higher ups and HR to play a critical role to provide inputs to identify right talents across the organization for grooming and nurturing talents for higher responsibilities to ensure growth and sustainability. HR has to take leadership role for change management to turn around eighty percent privilege seekers to performers so as to grow the pool of achievers.

In India, many industrial conglomerates in the private sector, who were dominant in 1960s, 1970s and even in the 1980s, were reduced to nonentities. Many such enterprises started by visionary predecessors have broken up due to family feuds, asset stripping, differing aspirations of factions not akin to business interest, money laundering, and missed potential growth opportunities.

A good to great organization sustains its competitive position by ensuring close linkages in leadership, structure, strategy, and culture. The culture of an organization developed over a period determines its ethos, ethics, core values, work style, and employee engagement in carrying out business objectives. Culture determines its orientation towards business transformation requiring initiative, mastering efficiency and innovative goals, and data driven objectives as a learning enterprise. Strategy stemming from the top management aligned with the corporate vision for growth and sustainability, is a plan of action designed to achieve organizational goals. A big strategy without focusing on the transformational need of work culture and required alignment and or adjustment in structure to achieve strategic objectives is likely to fail. Similarly evolving a new culture without recourse to a clear, compelling strategic direction, based on honesty and integrity, is risky and likely to cause disruptions. The linkage between strategy and culture is a matter of art. Both should be identified with the organization's competitive advantages, priotization of activities, and resource allocation in key capabilities, and must be supported by the management systems and processes to measure success. Here comes the role of leadership to steer the organization on the right path.

A leadership style that tends to control every level of a company is bound to fail. In 2024, Paul Graham , a Co-founder of Y combinatory, coined the term 'founder mode' to describe a style often adopted by promoters which leans heavily on individualism leading to authoritarian even abusive behavior.

Many organizations suffer from poor leadership style lacking vision not in synchrony with disruptive environmental demands. A leader has to be bold, knowledgeable, visionary, empathetic, and should be in a position to lead from the front by example so as to provide necessary stimuli across the organization. However, good strategies linked with operating culture and leadership style may not be sufficient unless the organizational structure is proper to provide roles and responsibilities with commensurate delegated authority and empowerment with accountability instead of top-down close structure. Depending upon size, scale of operations, geographical spread, nature of business, market, technology, etc., structure could be functional, divisional, profit or responsibility centric, matrix, or hybrid. Based on organizational growth and priorities, the right structure evolves over a period. Synthesis and alignment of all these success factors, viz. structure, strategy, culture, and leadership are complex and challenging, require close attention and monitoring and continuity of top leadership. Often we consider culture is the responsibility of HR and strategy to be developed by the operations team. Such an approach results in disconnect. In fact, strategy people should share emerging hypothesis, possibilities, and choices while the culture team outlines strengths, limitations and problems of existing culture so that there is proper integration of strategy and culture based on a common language for the employees to understand the direction of the organization. It is the role of leadership to remove latent inertia, laziness, and procrastination so as to build a sense of pride, motivation and required change management in attitude for achieving results.

In summary, a true leader has to be visionary, authentic, adaptive, knowledgeable, rational, a good strategist, motivator, empathetic and inspirational, a team builder, effective communicator, calm under disruptive situation, and capable of managing emotions of employees.

(Adapted from Author's own book "Journey Through the University of Life" published by Inkfeathers Publishing (www.inkfeathers.com) with appropriate changes in the narratives.)

2.
WHAT TYPE OF BOSS ARE YOU?

Being retired and somewhat idle, Author in an expansive mood started thinking more on this subject based on his past interactions with a number of persons, many of whom were his bosses, a few mentors whom he regards highly, and a large number of his subordinates with potentials.

During his professional journey over a span of more than forty years, Author came across several bosses to whom he used to report. Based on his interactions and experience he classified them in four categories:

- TORMENTORS,
- INHIBITORS,
- MOTIVATORS,
- INSPIRATIONAL & MENTORS.

The first category i.e. **Tormentors** are largest in numbers. This group derives sadistic pleasures often suffering from prejudices, biases, inferiority complex, and insecurity, in tormenting and humiliating their subordinates. They rise to respective positions through ranks and by virtue of proximity to their bosses and often being tormented earlier and in the course learned the tricks of subjugating subordinates. They generally tend to ignore new comers, however brilliant and qualified, and torment them with mediocre activities. If a subordinate brings a good idea for consideration, tormentor boss will ridicule and embarrass him with shouts often in presence of others questioning his knowledge and understanding of the subject. This is a sure shot to demoralize the person, who perhaps could have been his strength otherwise. Such behavior often results into departure of talented youngsters for opportunity elsewhere. They also use juniors for mundane personal work.

I have come across quite a few seniors using juniors to serve tea/coffee or drinks during any get together. In contrast, I had seen during a meeting in London with a senior executive of a reputed financial organization, himself made tea/coffee not only for the visitors but also for his assistant present in the meeting, That was not only inspiring but speaks about corporate culture.

Tormentor types do not motivate or believe in team work and generally tend to operate solo. This type destroys organizational culture and effectiveness.

Inhibitors, like Tormentors, try to inhibit the potential of subordinates by their superior attitude, even though their knowledge level is somewhat shallow. This class generally does not believe in employee engagement and empowerment. They will give unachievable tasks and timeframe to juniors, who after burning midnight oil when present best case scenario, instead of going through the presentation, ridicule the person with some sarcastic comments without giving any positive suggestion for refinement, if any, needed. If one probes deeply to find out ideas and thoughts on the matter from this group, they will fumble and demonstrate their lack of clarity and understanding. They tend to make false pretense of superior knowledge and understanding before their superiors. Such bosses equally harm the organization and tend to destroy performance and productivity. If such work culture pervades across the organization, the organization is bound to fail sooner or later.

Motivators type though less in number are real assets to any organization. They try to build up the team, engage their juniors with proper roles and responsibilities, often guiding them with suggestions and recommending way forward. They communicate effectively for better understanding of expectations from their subordinates. They try to bring in hidden potential of their juniors to strengthen the team and the organization. They value quality work and encourage and motivate juniors not only with guidance but with complimentary words creating a positive environment and work culture. Motivators significantly contribute towards development of human resources fostering growth and sustainability of the organization. They inculcate a sense of value based positive work culture and develop leadership traits among juniors to build up pipeline of future leaders. In such a situation organization moves forward with higher performance and results.

The last category i.e. **"Inspirational & Mentors"** are very few in any organization, who not only develop quality and committed teams, an essential component of organizational success, but build up future leaders for challenging assignments. They value human talents, demonstrate respectful behavior with the juniors to foster comradeship, provide guidance and encouragement with pat on the back attitude so as to bring out hidden talents of subordinates. They are usually empathetic to juniors, often operate out of their cubicles to supervise the work of the juniors more as guides and mentors. They tend to believe in delegation with accountability, but protect the juniors in the event of any oversight or mistake and encourages them to be careful as learning insight to avoid recurrence. This fosters loyalty, positive and value based work culture for improved performance.

The first two categories lack sensitivity, make the work environment more stressful destroying work culture resulting higher attrition of talents. They have a tendency to brag and boast about their own small achievements. These types believe in disengagement, political infighting, and support mediocrity. These type of executives operate in silos creating barrier between them and others, hindering synergy leading to duplicate efforts and missed opportunities. They destroy organizational effectiveness, and accelerate the process of organizational decay. Unfortunately, these categories of bosses are large in number in any organization and tend to get promoted to senior positions even with low performance but due to closeness to their bosses based on some trust relationship. In the long run such organizations populated by those quality of executives bound to decay.

The last two categories create value and build up the organization for success and growth so as to remain ahead of the pack. They treat their juniors sensitively, engage them in discussion to iron out any communication gap so as to achieve desired objectives. These types believe in positive reinforcement, behave as facilitators by providing clear direction, setting boundaries and preventing aggressive behavior which undermine morale and team effectiveness. They display humility and empathy. Organization having such motivators and mentors builds up loyalty, future leaders, corporate values for organizational success and growth.

It is the role of HR team and top leadership in any organization to monitor boss and subordinate relationship to build up right kind of operating work culture which foster harmony, career growth, balanced work culture, teamwork, and loyalty so as to improve productivity, efficiency and performance to remain competitive and ahead of the pack.

Invariably high performing organizations try to build up leadership pool by encouraging innovative mindset, freedom of operations with accountability, setting higher goals with appropriate monitoring systems and processes. HR processes in such organizations focused on value based work culture, building up suitable bridge between seniors and juniors to ensure proper mentorship.

We observe such inclusive and balanced behavior in some of the leading corporates in our country like Tata, L&T, Mahindra & Mahindra, ITC, HUL, IT Companies, just to name a few and a some of large companies under PSUs. These companies continuously strive for growth, sustainability, and balanced work culture with improved corporate governance and social responsibility.

3.
ORGANIZATIONAL CHAOS

Recently an US based multinational organization having global presence came under a major cyber-attack disrupting entire IT infrastructure including SAP and communications systems. Intruders hacked and accessed and infiltrated information systems. All computers were affected making the hardware and software inoperative. The organization was not ready with a plan B under such a situation. The firewall of IT infrastructure fell victim to the situation. As usual, there was panic reaction across the organization more at the senior echelon who were clueless how to sustain global service operations without much of disruptions. Major burden fell on IT department to rectify the situation as quickly as possible even though small IT operating team was equally clueless how to retrieve the situation. Though much of services were outsourced, the team members started operating day and night under stressful situation without sufficient rests and timely meals. The organization apparently did not have necessary support system to provide desired comfort and encouragement to the IT team. Because of panic reaction, bosses became more hyper and were on the toes of the juniors, who were in any case doing their best relentlessly, thereby creating more tension. The bosses behaved more as tormentor and inhibitor rather than supportive affecting morale and effectiveness of the team causing further chaos and delays.

It is a classic case of behavioral management and operating culture of the organization as revealed under a disruptive situation. Most of the seniors behaved more as tormentors and inhibitors thereby causing further avoidable chaos increasing stress level of the IT team members. The situation was brought under control after a few weeks of hard labor of all concerned taking some tolls on the health and family life of quite a few. During the process few of otherwise talented executives lost their jobs.

It's an ideal case study. What should be the cognitive behavior of the organization under such a disruptive situation?

Company A like the above goes into panic mode resulting charged atmosphere. Bosses tend to behave erratically with their subordinates with shouts and lack of empathy. Under such a situation, blame game and political infighting goes on and often juniors fell victim in such a situation. Seniors in order to protect their own back often navigate the situation by blaming juniors thereby accentuating the already charged atmosphere with negative consequences. More often than not, in such an organization seniors remain unreachable causing a fear psychosis among juniors. The juniors often find it difficult whom to turn for required guidance and cooperation thereby causing further confusion and delays. At the end, after retrieval of the situation, many may not find the work culture favorable and the organization an ideal place to work. Organization may lose some talents causing a set back with hidden costs on a long-term basis. The overall attitude and behavior in such disruptive situation reflect on the negative operating culture of the organization and may not be a happy workplace for employees leading to high attrition rate. It's a failure of HR function and leadership. This type of organizations becomes victim of disruptive scenarios loosing market shares and trust of the stakeholders and likely candidates for takeover by the competitors.

Company B under such a situation calmly assess the overall situation and build up fast track action plan with the involvement of key members and communicate to other team members what needed to be done. Senior managers manage the situation with encouragement and empathy with junior members to retrieve the situation as quickly as possible. They ensure positive work environment providing necessary rest and comfort as feasible to overworked employees under such a stressful situation so as to cause minimum disturbance to work – family life balance. In such a company senior members display a fellowship while working hand in hand with the juniors and participate in various decision making for sharing responsibilities instead of blame game. This company believes in bringing the problem on the table for an open and healthy debate, seek suggestions and feedbacks to arrive at a consensus in the work plan for effective implementation by allocating work responsibilities to various teams. After retrieval of the situation, leadership analyzes and reviews the lessons learnt for necessary preventive measures with necessary structural changes as required to avoid recurrence with checklists for guidance.

Company B compared to Company A believes in communication and try to create a positive work environment to avoid panic and more stresses and try to lead from the front by the seniors. They provide incentives to the team as further inducement not only to retain talents but also to build up loyalty and commitment. The role of leadership is very crucial in a disruptive situation. If we do not have a right kind of leadership who can make hard problems simple by asking difficult questions to find new ways bring required discipline in an adaptive manner, the crisis may persist.. The leadership has to show maturity in dealing with various situations including disruptive situations. Such organization continue to remain an ideal workplace and sustain its stability and growth in a competitive environment.

Chaos is quite common in organizations and good organizations generally have an action plan and strategies to mitigate failure and unpredictability in a disruptive situation. With rapid growth of technology, new products and competitions, IT systems built on artificial intelligence (AI), shifting markets, changing consumer behavior, etc. are often result into new challenges and disruptions in conventional way of doing business. Now a day's success depends on managing disruptions, quick adaptability, flexible strategies and work plan, tactical brilliance of key management personnel, and virtual monitoring of results for sustainability. Successful organizations in such an environment quickly adopt to changes required while addressing the situation by encouraging creativity, engaging employees, and learning from mistakes. Management in such organization are agile, resilient, and emphasize on flexibility and adaptability to manage the situation.

4. SOME THOUGHTS ON BUDGETARY PRACTICES

In most organizations, depending upon importance attached to the exercise, budgeting and budgetary control systems is a lengthy process of determining income and expenditures for planned activities and goals during a given period prepared in advance to manage operational and financial performances. As a part of budgetary control systems actual results are mapped against budgeted numbers to identify variances for corrective actions so as to achieve targeted results.

Objective of this article is not to espouse on well-read and articulated subject, as there are plethora of articles delving on budget and budgetary control systems by eminent authors, but to highlight some behavioral aspects of budget preparation more as an experience sharing.

In most of the organization, budget is top-down exercise setting goals and targets and bottom up for resource needs i.e. in a hybrid mode. Depending upon nature of business, scale of operations, diversity and geographical spread of businesses, resources are allocated based on assessed priorities and objectives of results to be achieved. In an ideal situation having a stable environment, actuals behaved more rationally with budgeted numbers. But we never face an ideal and stable environment. More often than not, there are shifting priorities due to changing environmental forces - market, technology, customer preferences, geopolitical events, govt. policies, etc. which make budgetary control system more complex and require to be monitored in a virtual mode.

Many progressive organizations try to align long-term plans – fixed or rolling, and strategies while framing budgets with in-built flexibility based on situation analysis to ensure least variances in budgeted targets and actual performances. Success depends on how robust is the budgetary exercise with built-in control mechanisms. Unfortunately, gaps emerge while trying to integrate resource demands of various stakeholders including cost, profit, business, and responsibility centers. Often business heads demand resources based on their areas of responsibilities, accountability and understanding of resource need. However, resource allocation through budget framing often gets influenced by perceived aggressiveness, personality, persuasive nature and position in the hierarchical structure of the organization by respective business heads. An aggressive business head and his team may demand more resource than actually needed, while a less aggressive business head might get less allocation not in conformity with his areas of responsibilities. In many organization senior people tend to operate in silos creating barrier for seamless operations. At times one-upmanship becomes a dominant virtue to create an individual mark and legacy which attitude may not be congruent with the desired organizational objectives and results become detrimental due to duplication, wastages and redundancies. It is up to the job of the budget controller at the corporate level to foresee such tendencies among individual stakeholders and deftly manage the situation while allocating budgetary resources strictly on the basis of prioritization of activities in the best organizational interest. To achieve this, leadership style, interpersonal relationship and behavioral pattern come into play. Ideally executive committee or top leadership should analyze the situation and involve such business heads to iron out differences to finalize the budget in the best interest of the organization.

However, it is easier said than done. For a large business conglomerate, the budgetary exercise becomes more complex and time consuming more particularly to ensure positive returns from various business verticals. To a large extent it is dependent on experience, expertise of the team finalizing the budget. Author had experienced gaps and failure at that level to meet the varied demands of resources from various stake holders to achieve business objectives. Since the budget required to be finalized and communicated before commencement of the budgeted period, with time pressure and last minutes adjustments often vitiates integrity and control measures of the intense exercise resulting large variances between budget and actuals. Even flexible budgets to mitigate such variances in actual behavior fall prey if business environment experiences turbulence, which is quite likely.

In a contemporary business environment with rapid changes in technology, software applications, control systems, markets, competitive scenario, etc. perceptive management try to upgrade the business model and systems and strategies for effective control of the situation and to achieve desired results. This calls for a learning and agile organization with right kind of leadership. From author's perspective, in a dynamic and evolving environment, structural changes may also be required with balanced delegation of authorities and responsibilities to achieve desired results. Accordingly budgetary control systems also required to be aligned with any structural changes for effectiveness and to avoid underutilization and overutilization of budgeted allocation of resources.

It is often seen mismatch of physical and financial performances mostly in project oriented organizations resulting cost and time overrun. To mitigate that, there should be continuous monitoring of resource utilization and physical performances for on time corrective measures to avoid lost opportunities based on post mortem. IT systems and processes should be reviewed as often as possible to see if desired MIS are being generated for review and required corrective measures almost virtually to achieve better results. Author believes that a learning and agile organization with committed leadership could manage behavioral aspects of the budgetary practices more effectively for desired results compared to others.

Budget framing and resource allocation is often dependent on at what stage and shape the organization is poised. For example, in a stagnated and/or declining phase of business life cycle, the organization must harness its available resources more judiciously based on cost evaluation avoiding redundancies and wastages to sustain business operations with an objective of business turnaround. Author however had observed that when the organization was going through difficult and challenging times putting pressure on top line and bottom line, management often remained oblivious with business as usual mentality with old routines of resource allocation through budgetary process thereby accelerating phase of business decline.

To illustrate, sharing author's experience in a leading energy PSU where he was engaged and in one of family owned listed medium sized Shoemaking Companies where he was one of Independent Directors.

The energy company has pan India presence and on a growth track since its inception. At any given point of time multiple projects are running in parallel both on onshore and offshore arenas. During early phases, budget preparation was manually computed and consolidated based on demands of resources from various projects often influenced by aggressiveness and influence of the then project heads for allocation of budgetary resources, though moderated by respective operational directors. This approach resulted underutilization and overutilization of allocations of capex (capital expenditure) often resulting capacity mismatch at various work centers. In fact Project Heads operating in silos depending upon perceived importance created physical facilities and procured resources which were later on found to be underutilized or surplus requiring disposal without much use. With improvement in systems and software applications things have improved considerably since early days, but behavioral aspects as highlighted above continue to remain a dominant influencing factor in resource allocation and utilization. With top management focus and proper prioritization of value creation across the value chain has however helped in streamlining resource utilization in budget detailing using SAP template to a large extent.

Coming to the illustration of family owned company, despite dominant presence in eastern part of the country with limited presence in other parts of the country, company is facing headwinds due to declining footfalls in retail outlets against the onslaught of digital online demands more from youngsters with changing fashion and design need of such clientele under intense market competition from other players. To cater to such changes, marketing initiatives require frequent adjustments in terms of product offerings, production and inventory management not only at factories but also at distribution centers and retail network. In the absence of close coordination among production head, marketing head, and CFO the company was found to be faltering at those levels leading to increased volume of raw materials, nonmoving and slow moving finished stocks at different places, putting pressure on working capital and inventory management impacting revenue and margins. Under such a situation budget exercise becomes very challenging which is often based on historical data, inputs and feedback from various work centers and sales outlets as well as strategies adopted under changed scenario. For seamless operation among procurement, manufacturing centers including outsourced agencies, and distribution and sales outlets to manage inventory and sales performance, company requires a robust management information system with necessary tools under strict watch by CEO & CFO based on appropriate KPIs for various responsibility centers and key management personnel entrusted with results. For high performance, it requires not only good strategies but also tactical brilliance of the key management personnel. Being a family run business with owners' mindset and priorities, the company was found to be faltering on various parameters set on budget. The actual results almost in all quarters' showed large variances reflecting declining revenue, shrinking bottom-line, and stressed working capital and fund management. This example highlights how budget exercise often becomes so challenging unless backed up by necessary tools and systems to derive intended results particularly under disruptive circumstances.

The disruptive environment with the advent of Artificial Intelligence, Robotics, and other technologies are transforming existing industries and spawning new ones. Under such a pace of change, conventional product – market strategies may result inefficient outcome. Budget framing also has to adapt to such a disruptive environment embracing capabilities needed for quick adjustments innovatively with the support of necessary systems, processes, and tools. Resource allocation should be need based and strategies adopted for optimum results based on virtual monitoring systems and templates so that corrective actions could be taken well in time if going was found off-track. In fact focused approach with good monitoring systems and tools under watch of able leaders yield better results even under disruptive situations.

5. ORGANIZATIONAL RESTRUCTURING – SOME PITTFALLS

During the life span of any organization it undergoes several structural changes keeping pace with the environmental changes and for desired strategic management. The scope of organizational restructuring often shaped by the business model, strategic priorities to make the organization more balanced, profitable for seamless operations. It also gets influenced by competitive landscape, technology changes, regulatory changes, management perspective, etc. A good structure is the one which best fit with the strategy to avoid confusion, misdirection and splintered efforts.

Most of large Organizations are a mix of complex system of mutually dependent parts. It is logical that any organizational change involved alteration or modification of one or more parts of the systems and subsystems. While organizations do undergo minor changes regularly depending upon growth and strategic priorities, major structural change(s) occur when business model and environmental dynamics demands an adjustments to remain competitive and sustainable in alignment with vision, mission, and objectives of the business. As observed, most of the organizations undergo quite a few need based transformative changes during the life span. Growth, mergers and acquisitions, business split-up or demergers also call for structural changes.

As a number of well- articulated write-ups, research papers, and literatures by eminent authors are available which will make the readers more enriched, objective of this article is more of an experience sharing and to bring out certain dichotomy and fallacies as observed during real life structural readjustments in an organization where author had the privilege to be engaged.

With growth and expansion of the organization it becomes imperative to have structural adjustments to make operations and functions more cohesive and efficient to achieve better results. A large business organization operating in several business verticals may find such restructuring exercise with in-house expertise a time consuming and a cumbersome process. Such an effort may not be a right fit exercise due to certain mental blocks, cultural prejudices, and lack of required updated knowledge. Large companies often engage one of well-known international consulting houses, viz. McKinsey, BCG, A. T. Kearney, Arthur D. Little, Deloitte, and others for the assignment and required handholding during recommended change implementation process.

However, question is whether such restructuring exercise with the help of external consultants at a substantial cost really provide desired results and benefits? Author found from his experience that it was not always so. Generally speaking, most of recommendations based on Consultants global templates arising out of their engagements elsewhere suggest shifting from functional, to business groups, to SBUs, to say, Asset – Basin model (for an energy company), or hybrid or matrix type for corporate and geographically spread out business units/entities with redistributed roles and responsibilities of key management personnel as per the recommended structure(s). The Consultant so engaged often interact with the senior management for better appreciation of vision, mission and strategies, etc. and core issues and bottlenecks hindering performance. Based on subsequent SWOT analysis and critical reviews, periodic discussion with the management team(s), consultant so engaged submit their recommendation(s) with proposed modified structure, blue print, guidelines, manual, etc. to the management. Depending upon scope of contractual responsibilities, consultants also handhold management team for smooth implementation of the revised structure, with SOPs, checklists, and needed change management discipline.

Author observed from his experience that external consultants often missed out working culture, formal particularly informal group structuring, and certain hard to eliminate established work practices developed over a period, and mid-level leadership quality which prima facie would be the key driver for implementing recommended restructuring and desired change management. As a result, even a well-meaning restructuring plan and model, once implemented do not give desired results for improved productivity, efficiency and profitability due to lack of communication, inertia, resistance to change mindset and behavioral changes needed at the working level.

During the span of author's engagement for two decades in a large geographically spread out Public Sector Energy Company, he observed at least two such restructuring exercises in that organization, from functional set up, to business group set up, to asset – basin model. Such transitions were influenced by respective CEOs during their time to make the organization more efficient, nimble, and profitable. The organization was functionally structured during growth phase of the life cycle. During this phase there was continuous volume and revenue growth due to newly discovered oil fields resulting improved top line and bottom line. However, growth of business and increased level of activities resulted setting up of new departments and added manpower. The then CEO felt the necessity of restructuring various business verticals for better cohesion and accountability for higher performance. The exercise was undertaken by an in-house core group under the leadership of the board. The functional group structure was converted into business group model. Each business group was headed by an experienced and senior executive directly reporting to the CEO having dotted line reporting to other functional directors for achieving budgeted targets and results. However this transformation with new reporting's under revised delegated powers did not, as observed by the author, result in dramatic improvement in performances. Business was being run as usual with historically established functional loyalty, performance evaluation and accountability.

It must be stated at this stage that idea of any critical review is not to undermine the efforts but more from learning perspective to understand why some restructuring do not yield desired results. While undertaking a restructuring we often miss out creating a robust MIS template to objectively evaluate benefits achieved vis-à-vis earlier structure. Otherwise, any such gains, if not measured, will be lost in the midst of business as usual mindset. Such measurement will give necessary impetus and confidence to the leadership about the success of the change undertaken and also to take further corrective measures needed to iron out any gaps in strategies, systems, and processes to achieve optimum results. Since no such objective review was undertaken, it cannot be stated with confidence that the change undertaken really improved overall performance, as the organization was on a growth momentum generating higher revenue due to volume growth from newly discovered offshore fields despite some volume decline in matured onshore producing fields. On a hindsight, it could be stated that business structure resulted somewhat bloated corporate structure both at headquarters and regions having many technical people operating from the offices to assist senior managers creating additional layers under the garb of management service groups. This also eventually resulted in top heavy structure under lopsided promotion strategies undertaken damaging decision making processes impacting organizational effectiveness and other subtle cultural shifts not conducive from the perspective of growth and sustainability.

Post 1990's the organization started facing new challenges – flattening and eventual start of decline of fields productivity in the absence of major discoveries and emerging competition from private players with change in Govt. policies in the sector. To contain decline and to sustain field productivity large capital investments were undertaken for incremental gain in production resulting higher marginal cost and reduced return on investments. The then management felt the need for another restructuring to improve performance and to sustain growth momentum. Towards end of 1990's, a globally well-known consulting house was engaged for the same. After detailed study and review with the senior management, the consultants recommended restructuring the organization under Asset – Basin model as followed by many large global energy companies elsewhere. The existing producing fields were brought under several groups as assets while predominantly exploratory fields were considered as basins. Each asset class was brought under the charge of an Asset Manager, while each basin was headed by Basin Manager. Depending upon size and scale of operation, each asset and basin managers were provided team of specialist manpower along with support services. Existing manpower was redistributed as per the new structure with revised delegated powers.

Unlike other global oil majors where majority services like survey, data processing, drilling, cementing, logging, maintenance, civil works, etc. are outsourced keeping core activities internally, the Indian Company since inception and due to historical reasons built up in-house capabilities for such services thereby becoming an integrated exploration and production company. The company outsourced certain services from time to time to augment resource need over and above in-house capabilities. As such there was a need for evaluating and comparing performances of in-house services with those of outsourced services to measure benefits accruing through reorganized structure. It was also equally necessary to identify loss making businesses and operations to prioritize resource allocation to optimize performance. This calls for a robust management information system for efficient comparison and to ensure productive uses of in-house and outsourced resources as well as to identify loss making units and operations for necessary corrective actions. Author observed that this aspect was missed out in the final recommendation of the consultants. In the absence of such comparison and required measurement tools, it cannot be stated with confidence that modified structure since implemented did give superior results. Incidentally, in February 2002, domestic crude oil price was deregulated from regulated pricing regime during this phase of reorganization. The domestic oil companies started receiving international oil prices on its production. This resulted windfall gain in revenue and bottom line due to upward trend of international oil prices influenced by geopolitical reasons and OPEC decisions. Thus better financial results as observed in subsequent years cannot straightway be attributed to reorganized structure and management strategies adopted. Against the onslaught of declining field productivity of matured fields and to arrest the decline there was large capital spending and increased dependence on outsourced services with gradual neglect of in-house capabilities and assets. The increase in costs on various operating parameters got obfuscated due to higher prices being received on its produces due to external factors despite production decline which could not be supplemented through improved or enhanced recovery through additional capital investments and production from new small and marginal discoveries. Economic value addition was also not commensurate with the capital spending. Besides, manpower from various support services like Finance, HR, Material procurement, Maintenance, Logistics, etc. which earlier were under the charge of respective Functional Directors got distributed under Asset and Basin Managers on need based requirement. This resulted shifting loyalties to their new bosses with subtle behavioral changes in such redistributed employees, depending upon personality and leadership styles of such Asset and Basin managers, perhaps to meet career growth aspirations which may not always be conducive to professional ethics and judgment required in the best interest of the organization. Such changes and consequences on organizational results are often difficult to ascertain in the absence of an objective and impartial evaluation system at different levels.

The above observation of gaps in high profile consultants' engagement got reinforced from example of another leading organization in the banking sector under PSU. The retired CEO of the bank during a flight where the author and the CEO were co-passengers, expressed similar views and organization frustration when the bank got reorganized on the basis of recommendations of the same leading global consultant so engaged. He expressed his disappointment about consultants' limited skill base to recognize organizational ethos, culture, and internal dynamics while trying to implement their recommendations across the organization. It became a chaotic change process absorbing much more management time and final outcome was not on expected lines.

A forward looking management always try to keep pace with changes required to remain competitive and to sustain growth. This calls for management focus on performance evaluation, HR policies, system improvement and leadership development on an ongoing basis. Without that focus and attention, organization performance even after restructuring might get stymied obfuscating results and gains. Leadership also has to take care of cultural changes required by employees to adopt to changes based on restructuring to bring in higher performance. This area is difficult and complex and could be a slow process to change mindset, inertia and attitude of resistance to change. HR development and monitoring will be key success factors for managing such transition and leadership should remain focused with appropriate measurement templates to achieve success and better results otherwise might not yield intended benefits through restructuring.

6.
WHY STRATEGIES FAIL?

Most of the organizations - large, medium, small, or start up – try to put their strategies in place for success. Strategy is long-term plans to achieve organizational goals and objectives in line with vision and mission of the organization. It outlines how the organization should allocate its resources and develop capabilities to pursue its business.

Depending upon nature, scale, types, spread of business, strategic focus varies from organization to organization. Again based on vision, mission and SWOT analysis, competitive position, etc. strategic focus could either be cost leadership, market leadership, growth and business sustainability, new product – new market opportunities, or combination of all these. Holistically speaking corporate and business strategies aim to deliver,

- Optimum utilization of resources,
- Profit maximization and risk mitigation,
- Long-term growth and sustainability for competitive advantage,
- Vertical or horizontal integration of businesses,

- Structural changes for seamless operations,
- Merger / demerger, Acquisition of new business,
- Focus on innovation and R & D,
- And so on.

While there are large number of articles, research papers, and case studies elaborating on Corporate and business strategies, we shall try to understand more from macro perspective, why many well thought-out and planned strategies fail to deliver desired results. This is not a case study but outlines broad contour of causes of failures.

Before we get into above theme, it would be interesting to understand strategies followed by some economically strong countries like Japan, Germany, and South Korea. All those countries were devastated during Second World War or war in Korean peninsula. These countries are not endowed with fossil fuel, or many essential minerals, but still became economic giants rebuilding the nation in a span of few decades from huge human, economic, and infrastructure devastation and catastrophy.

Japan's post war miracle is due to strategic Government-Industry collaboration, rapid industrialization, technological innovation, and investment in R&D especially in robotics, automation, electronics, and material sciences, with strategic focus on export –oriented growth. Japan invested heavily in education, developing a highly skilled, disciplined, and technologically adept workforce. The concept of 'Kaizen' i.e. continuous improvement, Lean manufacturing, Just in Time support system in manufacturing, etc. helped Japanese companies to focus on efficiency, reduce waste and enhance product and service quality. Country's economy thrived due to strong brands, economies of scale, portfolio of intellectual properties, product design capabilities, human capital advantages, etc. Besides, love for the country by citizens, loyalty and pride helped Japan to become an economic giant.

Germany, similarly, became an economic powerhouse by combining industrial strength, strong institutions, and a highly skilled labour force. Post war Germany embraced a Social Market Economy with a balanced approach towards market competition and social welfare. The currency reform adopted in 1948 benefited and stabilized the economy. Like Japan, Germany's strategic focus is on manufacturing and exports. Over a period it created strong institutions and infrastructure by combining vocational training and apprenticeships which helped creating a highly skilled workforce aligned with the needs of its industries.

Similar strategies were followed by South Korea – Government played an active role on rapid industrialization, infrastructure development, and export promotion. South Korea supported large family owned conglomerates famously known as 'Chaebols' like Samsung, Hyundai, Daewoo, and LG all of which created global brands.

Key strategies common to all above three countries were export oriented growth, planned Government support and intervention, infrastructure investment, education and workforce development, automation and technological advancement through focus on R&D which helped all these countries to build up strong manufacturing base with focus on global leadership of goods and services. Their ability to adapt, invest in infrastructure, build strong institutions, and strong achievement motivation were key factors in their rise to global economic powers.

Later on similar strategies were followed by China for its economic miracle.

Objective of giving a snap shot of these economic giants is to understand strategies adopted by these countries for economic success. Following those strategies these countries established number of corporate giants and global brands.

Major Corporates worldwide follow similar strategies to build up critical mass and success stories. Organizational success, sustainability and growth to a large extent depend on vision, mission, strategies adopted, leadership style, HR policies, innovation, culture, and organizational structure to implement chosen strategies. It is critical to review strategies periodically to achieve optimum results.

However, despite good and sound strategies companies flounder for a variety of reasons. Often poor execution by the operating team due to lack of required focus and commitment, lack of necessary support system and resources, which become impediments in delivering desired results.

Besides, strategies can fail if they are too rigid to adapt to changing market scenario and new challenges. Success of strategy implementation to a large extent depends on effective leadership. If strategies and implementation plans are not adequately communicated to the operating teams, it may lead to failures. Hence communication to all stakeholders is one of key ingredients, failing which it can lead to confusion, misaligned efforts and failures. Failure of strategies can also be due to inherent complexities beside rigidity, leading to mistake or delays. Simple, focussed strategies tend to be more successful than overtly complicated ones.

It is also observed that good strategies failed due to resource constraints resulting from inadequate allocation of resources. Misaligned organizational structure, work culture, and resistance to change mind-set, can be major barriers for successful implementation of strategies. If role and responsibilities are not well defined and communicated, it may undermine strategy's effectiveness during implementation. In this context, the role of leadership is very crucial for monitoring and measurement of success at every stage and to take timely corrective measures if activities are found to be off the track. It is therefore imperative to identify key performance indicators (KPIs) and regular monitoring with the help of a robust management information system (MIS). Overconfidence or complacency on the part of executing teams may result potential hazards or obstacles and missing out on important external factors like economic downturns, regulatory changes, shift in market and consumer behaviour, software disruption, etc. leading to ineffective implementation of strategies.

Many organization suffer due to ambitious strategies to deliver results within a short span of time without required organizational structure, adequate resources and support systems. So while drawing out strategies, top management should map out potential hazards and risk factors in implementation and prepare the organization with right kind of teams, systems and processes and monitoring system for success.

In summary, while a good strategy is crucial, its success depends on strong leadership, proper execution, adaptability, and the ability to navigate both internal and external challenges.

In their book "Built to Last" Authors James C. Collins and Jerry I. Porras had indicated that visionary companies, as identified in their research work, were successful over a long period not necessarily based on brilliant and complex strategic planning, but by experimentation, trial and error, opportunism and often achieving success by accident. These companies followed several objectives besides creating shareholders wealth or profit maximization. These companies were found successful based on superior returns compared to competitors over a long period not primarily beating the competition, but through continuous improvements (like Kaizen principle of Japan) of their product and services. The Authors also found that during life cycle of selected visionary companies, they faced several challenges and setbacks but recovered based on strong urge to do better tomorrow and required flexibility to manoeuvre changed circumstances.

So strategic failures need not necessarily mean end of the road but how quickly one retrieves the situation through organizational strength, strategic flexibility, and bold decision making. In fact there are many things which matter in achieving business success which vary from organization to organization. It is imperative to communicate success factors of strategies to all key management personnel for achieving results.

Author had seen from his personal experience that objectives and strategies in PSUs were often influenced by Governments policies and priorities which may not always be in the best interest of the organization. The top management often succumb to the dictates of the concerned Minister(s) and Secretaries from owners' perspective. As a result, many factors which influence organizational performance like, capital spending, fund raisings, dividend distribution, business expansion, etc. are prioritised based on such dictates impacting optimum results. As a result return on investments is not optimal and organization suffers in the long run.

So is the case with family owned businesses where promoters' greed and tendencies of quick returns often disrupts the business model and strategies with harmful results. There are so many business failures both in India and abroad. Author came across story of one of such leading US based multinational service companies poised to take over another service company in the same domain but was prevented due to local competition regulations. Later on the same service company which was poised for a takeover became not only highly successful but a much bigger player by exploiting available market opportunities and implementing better strategies. In India, tractor business of Mahindra & Mahindra saw a downturn during early decade of this century and was rumoured to be taken over by another reputed auto company, but subsequently focussed strategies, new business model and bold leadership turnaround the company and has now become one of leading business conglomerates.

Among some leading PSUs bold and planned strategies helped them to grow and build up critical masses. For example, a leading energy PSU during early 2000 took over a loss making joint venture downstream company and turned it around through judicious mix of capital investment, leadership changes and forward looking strategies. There are several such success stories both in PSUs and Private sectors demonstrating implementation of good strategies for business growth.

Thus well thought-out strategies and bold leadership help organization to turn around and make it successful and sustainable.

7. WHY SOME ORGANIZATIONS DECAY RAPIDLY?

If we scan business horizon, we come across several organizations which started with bold vision, strategies and promises fade rather quickly and go for insolvency thereby causing economic loss and hardship to stakeholders. While objective of this article is not a research work but to get a glimpse of various factors causing such setback.

Objective of any organization is to grow and sustain business model for economic benefit to stakeholders. To achieve such objective, business enterprises carry out SWOT analysis to identify potential growth opportunities for new investment. Large organizations generally operate on several business segments often geographically spread out with varying strategies and business model. Resources get distributed depending upon scale, size, and nature of business and priorities identified.

Since the subject chosen is vast and varied and there are several academic and research work, I shall try to confine myself on a few aspects based on my experience and understanding. It is observed that a number of organizations, both large and medium, aspired to grow rapidly in different business segments for corporate success. However, rapid growth often leads to spreading their resources either too thin or increasing leverage through excessive borrowings. It is also a common strategy to leverage resources of a profitable entity within the group to support or piggyback another new or not so profitable entity within the group. It may be a good strategy to support financially a new venture, or a start-up, a subsidiary, or a joint venture in the group during initial phases of business stabilisation, but should not be a prolonged support at the cost of undermining balance sheet strength of the parent company. More particularly if such financial support from the parent company results additional borrowing thereby increasing the gearing of the parent company, it might impair its financial position with cascading impact on the market sentiment. For listed entities it become imperative to monitor market responses on such strategies. It is the role of CFO (Chief Finance Officer) to analyse impact of such funding to other group entities, contribution being made by such entities, and how it is impacting the parent company's profitability.

Unfortunately, resource distribution often get influenced by the decision of the promoter(s), majority shareholders influence on the board thereby suppressing prudent views of CFO in many organization resulting commencement of business decay. Many organizations particularly in the private sector, funds from one business get laundered into other businesses for rapid growth causing financial distress to all. Often short term borrowings are ploughed into capital projects of longer tenure impacting loan repayment defaults and rising interest obligations. This is due to lack of oversight by the management, audit committee, and the board of the company. It is the role of CFO to monitor end use of borrowed funds and company's ability to service debt without defaults and bring crucial analytical information to the board and audit committee for debate and critical review before a decision.

Author has observed from annual reports of a premier (Maharatna) Govt. undertaking that the parent company is subsidising various activities including guarantees on bank funding of the subsidiaries and joint venture companies of the group resulting reduction in profit margin as reflected in the consolidated statement vis-à-vis standalone financial statement. Due to large revenue and profit numbers in consolidated statement, financial results often obfuscate such details at the macro level unless analysed thoroughly, since a few of subsidiaries were having lower profitability or couple of them were lossmaking with inadequate return on capital employed. If this trend persists over a longer duration, chances are that the parent company might get exposed to financial distress unless rectified.

Another trend followed by many group companies is merger and demerger for short term gains but having long term negative consequences impacting stability of the merged or demerged entities. Unless such strategy is aimed towards sustainable growth of the business and monitored carefully, it is likely to lead to eventual decay.

While engaged in a global family owned business conglomerate, author came across a scenario where promoters decided to merge two unrelated medium size listed companies headquartered at different work centres with the objective of building a large size company to achieve better debt equity ratio of the merged entity having flexibility of meeting future fund requirements. On a hind sight it was observed that the valuation undertaken of the companies were skewed more to meet board and regulatory processes. The slightly smaller entity was merged into the relatively bigger one with a reconstituted single board. Post-merger the merged entity faced several challenges. The product and services of the two companies were totally different without any synergy. Besides there were differing cultural issues, and interpersonal issues. CEO of the merged entity was not comfortable with reporting to CEO of the combined entity. For all practical purposes, former with his team started working more or less independently with covert support from some family members of the group. Thus, while on paper both the companies got merged, at the operating level there was disharmony and lack of synergy. Eventually after a few years, it was decided to demerge to bring back premerger situation of two separate board managed listed companies. The merger carried out in haste did not result anticipated gains and perhaps loss of values. Many organization suffer from such ill-conceived strategic approach not based on merits and causes organizational decay.

Another factor which often tarnish the image and potential opportunities is higher valuation for short term gain. Author came across a privately owned medium size company which decided to go for an IPO and listing for business growth and better governance practices. The company had some funding from a fund house which after a couple of years got converted into equity funding. Objective of the fund house was to offload their stake during IPO to maximise gain from their investment. Based on a valuation carried out by external consultants, issue price was pegged at a much higher level than considered reasonable and initial price offering was high. After some aggressive road shows and marketing by the fund managers, the offer managed to get fully subscribed through participation of angel investors and public. Post listings, the prices fell considerably from offered price in the market causing significant losses to investors except the fund house which reaped major gain. Situation has not improved since then with trading prices hovering below 50% of the initial purchase price. Due to business stagnation, underlying business model, and rising costs, the company's profitability shrunk and the company skipped dividend payment to shareholders since issue barring one year. With negative market sentiments prices have not gained much resulting significant erosion of investors' wealth. If the situation does not improve through rigorous scrutiny of business model, underlying business fundamentals and strategies to overcome the negative sentiment, the company is bound to fail and decay. This is not a solitary case. Statistically speaking, around 25% of IPOs are found to be successful and enhance investors gain. Fundamental causes for such dismal results are many, could be due to bad planning, higher business valuation, bearish market sentiment, etc.

There are many other examples of business decline both in India and elsewhere. Some of these business declines were caused by promoters' greed for rapid growth by opening several business fronts simultaneously by spreading resources either too thin or trying to piggyback on profitable businesses within the group. On a post analysis, it was observed that business models, growth momentum and strategies were not sustainable due to resource crunch, dishonest practices, wrong strategies, and faulty financial planning.

Organizational decay does not occur overnight. Various factors like business model, organization structure, leadership, competitive mind set, strategies, core values and work culture, HR policies, technology, changed market scenario, brand, innovation, etc. build over a period make an organization sustainable. Neglect or oversight in any or more of these factors over a period starts a slow process of organizational decline. It is like termites which when infect a wooden furniture, slowly destroys the strength of the infected furniture before it falls apart. One has to take preventive measures well in time to avoid such a situation. This is equally true for an organization, where erosion of core strengths, business fundamentals and other early signals often get neglected which lead to stagnation and enterprise decay and eventual closure or change of hands of the enterprise. In most organizations middle level executives are the key drivers for strategy implementation, change management, and business growth. However, this layer is also most vulnerable in many organization as they are squeezed between top leaderships' watchful eyes for results and expectations of lower rungs for direction and guidance. For any down sight in business performance, they are first to go and remain under pressure. A perceptive and forward looking management protects, retain and nurture good talents at the middle level and also remain watchful about those early signals and take preventive measures well in time to ensure growth and sustainability of the organization.

8.
HOW EFFECTIVE IS CONTEMPORARY CORPORATE GOVERNANCE?

Corporate governance embraces the way a company is being managed not only for the benefit of its shareholders, but also to other stakeholders including every aspect of its relationship with the society. Importance of corporate governance was stimulated due to alleged fraud and mismanagement in some major UK and US companies and resultant failures of several large companies during late 80s and 90s. In 1992 the Cadbury Committee established a code of best practice for UK companies. Several countries followed with mandatory guidelines for better corporate governance practices for openness, integrity, and accountability. These guidelines emphasizes companies to present a balanced and understandable assessment of the company's financial position and likely prospects in the annual report. In the United States following the collapse of Enron, WorldCom, and others due to non-disclosure of off balance sheet exposures impacting financial health and stability of those organizations, Sarbanes Oxley Act was enacted to improve investor confidence and encourage full and transparent corporate reporting. In India, in 1999 SEBI established the Kumar Mangalam Birla Committee to recommend ways to improve corporate governance standards in listed companies. Since then besides all listed companies many private companies have also adopted some of best practices to improve transparency and accountability of various governance reporting.

The primary goal of corporate governance is to ensure that companies are managed in a way that enhances shareholder value while ensuring fairness, transparency, ethical conduct, accountability, and effective decision making. Transparency refers to the clear, accurate, and timely disclosure of all material information, enabling shareholders to assess the company's performance and make informed decisions. Corporate boards must be accountable for the company's performance and actions. In other words management of the company is held responsible for strategic direction and operational results. Corporate governance oversight should ensure that all shareholders' including minority shareholders are treated equitably and their rights are respected and interests are protected. Effective corporate governance also should ensure that companies profit making strategies matches with legal, ethical and social obligations. Corporate governance principles are expected to be fortified by presence of independent directors on the board of all listed companies who do not have ties to management or major shareholders to ensure unbiased decision making and avoid conflict of interests. In fact to ensure desired independence, effectiveness, and integrity of the board, there are regulatory prescriptions for board constitution. Independent directors are supposed to play vital role in maintaining objectivity, questioning management decisions including compensations to key management personnel, and reducing conflict of interests. Under corporate governance principles oversight by the audit committee is very important which focuses on financial reporting, internal controls, various regulatory compliances, and risk management to mitigate fraud or mismanagement. For effective role and contribution, audit committee is mostly comprised of independent directors of the board. Audit committee and the board should navigate issues related to data privacy, cyber security and digital ethics besides overseeing integrity of financial reporting.

Governance structure of any company must ensure shareholders participation in key decisions, such as directors' appointment, managerial remuneration, or approval of major transactions including mergers, demergers, acquisitions, etc. as per various provisions of the company's act and other regulations.

Despite importance given to corporate governance in recent time, there are gaps in its implementation by various companies. Major decisions are often get influenced by the promoters or majority shareholders which may not always be in the best interest of all stakeholders. Independent views or judgement of independent directors are often get subdued by the strong presence of promoters and their cohorts on the board. Unless there is ethical governance culture and top management believes in its inner philosophy, chances are that it would be more on paper for public consumption. Despite various guidelines and regulations, choice of independent directors on the board are often based on connection and closeness to the promoters group. It is true that promoters would like to have known persons on their boards as independent directors to ensure avoidable disputes during passage of important agendas in the board which from their perspective important and critical for company's growth and sustainability. Many boards however suffer from a lack of independence with directors being too closely tied to management or major shareholders thereby influencing board decisions which may not be in the best interest of the shareholders particularly that of minority shareholders. In listed PSUs apart from nominee directors on the board by concerned ministries, there are independent directors appointed by the government as owners, who are loyal and closely tied up with governing political party(ies), This can undermine the board's ability to provide unbiased oversight and effective checks on executive power. Unfortunately, it often becomes some kind of coterie more in family run businesses with the motto "you scratch my back and I scratch your back". Such approach dilutes the real effectiveness of independent directors. Barring some highly professionalised and/or multinational companies, corporate governance have not been ingrained in many. This is being stated going by reported failures of large number of companies either going for bankruptcy in USA (Chapter 11) and in other countries or insolvency in India as reported from time to time. We have seen failure of some mega corporates despite presence of some high profile personalities drawn from well-known universities and other professions on their boards as independent directors. Closure look of such failures reveal not only mismanagement, greed, lost opportunities, but also due to frauds, misuse of funds, ambition for rapid growth, market manipulation, etc. often disregarding prudent judgements of independent directors on the board. Independent directors on the board were found to falter on such cases of corporate failures either due to oversight or meekly submitting to various proposals brought before the board without detailed risk analysis and resultant impact of such proposals on financial stability of the company. Thus real accountability often gets misplaced.

Incidentally, effectiveness of independent director to a large extent depend on matters brought before periodic meetings of the board and information furnished for review and discussion. Major strategies and day to day management rest with the CEO, executive members of the board and other key management personnel. If selectively or inadequate information brought before the board, independent directors may not be wise enough to understand and follow issues which might impact on the performance and compromise corporate governance. Many a times critical and important proposals are brought to the board's attention at the last moment without enough time for proper deliberation and somewhat rushed through diluting the required need for risk evaluation. While audit committee deliberation may mitigate various risk aspects, to a large extent it depends on the knowledge, and inquisitiveness of the independent directors to seek additional information to do justice to various proposals brought before the board for consideration, if need be deferring the decision at the first go seeking additional information. Well governed companies tend to perform better in the long run. Effective oversight, ethical approach, and transparent decision making help ensure that companies focus on sustainable growth, profitability, and ethical business practices. Good governance signals to investors that the company values transparency and accountability.

Unfortunately, despite importance to corporate governance, there are several challenges in its effective implementation. Interests of key executives more particularly that of executive compensation may influence decision making for short term gains at the cost of shareholders interest from long term perspective. Corporate governance is often tested during trying times or scandal as happened with the failure of Enron, an energy giant, due to fudging profitability through nondisclosure of off balance sheet items and share price manipulation or failure of Lehman Brother, a globally reputed investment bank in 2008, during sub-prime crisis despite presence of high profile independent directors on the board. Enron episode also brought down one of large accounting firms, Arthur Anderson, because of conflict of interests. In India, in 2015, Satyam Computers one of the then successful IT companies collapsed due to personal greed of the founding brothers, fund embezzlement and accounting fraud. There are many such instances.

There are at times argument against corporate governance for over regulations and too prescriptive creating avoidable bureaucracy and compliance costs. Such critics argue that overly stringent governance rules may stifle innovation, discourage entrepreneurship, and reduce corporate flexibility.

Corporate governance practices can also vary across countries and cultures, leading to inconsistencies in expectations and practices. In some places it may be focussed more on short term financial returns, while in some other countries, long term value creation and stakeholder engagement take precedence. Critics argue that any narrow focus on profits has led to inequality, environmental degradation, and other societal inequity. What is required is a more holistic approach, where the interest of all stakeholders are considered as major governance practices. For effective and robust corporate governance practices are still evolving and board performances are often get tested with the presence of committed, experienced, and knowledgeable independent directors on the board who value their role with sincerity and integrity.

9.
MANAGEMENT PARADOXES

Recently a viral what Sapp video was in circulation in which Mr. Donald Trump is shown extolling employees and I am reproducing verbatim his alleged quote:

"Your job is not your life, it's just a job. I can explain. I shall explain the reason.

1) Your company is not your family. Companies exist primarily for profit and are not responsible for your personal wellbeing. No matter how much they promote family culture, their focus is business.

2) Your colleagues are not your friends. Keep in mind that people have their own interests and motivations Don't expect everyone to act in your best interest.

3) You are replaceable. If something bad happens to you, your company will find a replacement without hesitation. That's how businesses operate. It's not personal, it's business.

4) Don't fall for corporate propaganda. Companies often try to create an emotional bond to make you feel loyal. But this only benefits them. This tactics can trap you

into overworking and sacrificing your health for their gain.

5) Come to your workplace, do your job, get paid and go home. Remember that there is more to life than just your career."

The above statements are naked truth about corporate work culture particularly in USA.

Recently, one of very prominent and well respected co-founder of a well-known IT company in India extolled India's young to work 70 hours' per week in corporates, which transforms to 14 hours per day work in 5 days weekly work schedule in a week or about 12 hours per day in a six days per week, so that country can compete with the best globally.

Another head of a leading business conglomerate viewed that 8 hrs. stay at home may be disturbing at home front and may not be liked by the spouse. In other words, he is advocating longer stay of employees at work place, so that company gains and makes more profit for owners benefit.

Another head of a large engineering company wished his employees work on Sundays and 90 hours a week so as to maintain country's superiority globally. This view generated debate in media as well as trolled by many.

All the above statements or views are from very successful people from their exalted position and ivory tower mentality disregarding quality over quantity and its impact on employees' health and family disturbances. They appear to lack empathy and perceive their employees as robots without feelings and emotions. In the era of AI, a favourable work culture and innovative thinking are required as a contrast to working hours, which propel the organization and country to greater heights. Unfortunately, rich and successful business leaders often put the butt of the gun on the shoulders of overworked employees so as to generate more profits for their own benefits while paying peanuts to workers, and junior and middle level executives. We often see huge compensation packages for CEOs and top management personnel in the corporate sector widening the gaps of compensation disparities between both classes. Do they believe that work overload leading to employee burnout is the right way to move forward to achieve corporate excellence?

In 1926, Henry Ford introduced a 40 hour workweek with weekends off, promoting employee wellbeing and increasing leisure for use of cars. His decision significantly shaped modern labour practices and popularizes the concept of the weekend. He also doubled his workers' wages.

Going by various statistics in public domain, in USA and other European Countries average working hours per week is around 40 hours +/- 5 hours. In order to provide necessary comfort to employees, companies there adopt various means like flexible hours, congenial office environment, places for meditation, relaxation within office premises, etc. Such companies still flourish with innovative and superior products and services globally.

Does above position highlighted at the beginning reflect contemporary HR thoughts on work-life balance, and management principles of organizational development as propounded by various management gurus and thought leaders mostly from Ivy League management schools from western world? Unlike material sciences, management thought processes have evolved through empirical studies and observations by various management experts over a period in different corporate and industrial settings. In fact contemporary thoughts in Human Resources (HR) and Organizational Development (OD) have evolved significantly shifting from traditional transactional models to more dynamic, employee centric and more holistic approaches under the pressure of social, economic, technological changes and evolving employee expectations. New thoughts are on employee engagement, leadership, organizational culture, values, talent management, and adaptability. Contemporary management philosophies emphasize the importance of employee engagement moving away from autocratic top-down leadership to more participative and inclusive management style for driving employee motivation, morale, satisfaction, and retention. When HR and OD strategies align with contemporary management thoughts, organization achieves higher level of employee commitment, ownership thinking in decision making, and productivity and efficiency improvement for better results. This calls for value based cultural shift. Modern management thinking stresses the need for adaptive, transformational leadership that is both people oriented and results driven. OD practices now focus more on building leadership competencies moving away from traditional command and control practices, and emphasizing emotional intelligence, inclusivity, and collaborative leadership. A positive, inclusive, and innovative work culture is becoming central to attracting and retaining top talents. This requires organizational culture change which is a slow process and a challenge to implement. Contemporary management thinking places more focus on employee well-being, work-life balance, mental health, and flexibility to perform at their optimum.

Unfortunately, while we emphasize on modern management concepts and applications, at the implementation level we fail to acknowledge value creation through employee wellbeing. Having said that, let us look into various management and corporate paradoxes in contemporary business environment.

Management paradoxes, defined as situation where contradictory elements coexist in the same decision making environment, are increasingly acknowledged in modern organizational theory and practice. These paradoxes are inherent in the complexities of leadership, organizational dynamics, and decision making processes. They represent the tension between seemingly opposing forces that managers must navigate to sustain organizational effectiveness. Paradoxes such as balancing short term performance with long term goals, centralization with decentralization, and innovation with stability are just a few examples of this contradictory terrain. Understanding and addressing these paradoxes is crucial for both theory and practice in the realm of management.

We shall try to highlight some core paradoxes in management in this brief article.

- **Efficiency vs. Innovation:** one of the most fundamental paradoxes in management is the tension between maintaining operational efficiency and fostering innovation. Organizations are often under pressure to optimize current operations, streamline processes, and maximize productivity through employee engagement. However, innovation – whether in products, or processes – require an element of risk and experimentation, which can disrupt efficiency and may lead to inefficiencies at least for some time. This paradox forces managers to find a balance between sustaining the existing systems and fostering a culture that encourages creativity and new ideas. Question is does overworked environment fosters that kind of commitment and innovation? It's a myth going by various corporate failures. In fact, many successful organizations permit employees to experiment with new ideas which might cause temporary disruptions in regular workflow, but beneficial in the long run with discovery of blue ocean strategies, new products and services. The company like 3M, Sony, Apple, Tesla, etc. maintain their competitive edge and leadership position by maintaining a balance between efficiency and innovation as a part of corporate culture.

- **Control vs. Autonomy:** another prevalent paradox lies in the balance between control and autonomy. While organizations need to establish rules, procedures, and structure to ensure efficiency and coordination, they also need to empower employees with autonomy. Too much control can stifle innovation and demoralize employees, while too much autonomy may lead lack of alignment with organizational objectives and may lead to chaos. Leaders must navigate seemingly contradictory approaches and balance control and autonomy in the best interest of the organization. Thus there should be judicious balance between application of Theory X and Theory Y principles. It must be appreciated that corporate culture evolves over a period to sustain a balance between control and autonomy depending on belief and aspirational attitude of the organization through a process of trial and error.

- **Centralization vs. Decentralization:** the paradox between centralization and decentralization involves distribution of control mechanism within the organization. While centralization leads to better coordination and consistency but it may slow down decision making processes and creativity at lower levels. Decentralization on the other hand enhances responsiveness and flexibility but risk of misalignment in functioning. Managers are often confronted with determining how much control at the top vis.-a-vis. delegation to lower levels in the organization depending upon context, scale, accountability, and nature of business. Large organizations attempt to centralise some of the major activities like material procurements to take advantage of economies of scale, HR policies for uniformity, financial systems and processes for effective control, while approaching decentralized and flexible work ethics in manufacturing and operations. The adversarial impact of this paradox i.e. centralization vs. decentralization is mitigated by evolving work culture through trial and error for optimum results. As a compromise, many organizations attempt to centralise high value activities including centralise procurement while decentralise operational activities for efficiency and required flexibility.

- **Short term vs. Long term:** Organizations often face the paradox of balancing short-term objectives like quarterly results and targets with long-term strategies like sustainability, market expansion, or innovation. Pressure on achieving short-term goals for the benefit of shareholders and investors over long term investments, can undermine future success. It's quite a challenge to balance immediate needs with long-term strategic planning. Many organizations fail in managing the situation at the cost of organizational decline. There are a good number of corporate examples where short term priorities have overtaken long term vision and objectives thereby causing organizational decay. Many organization used funds borrowed for working capital management were found to have deployed for capital projects resulting mismanagement and default of debt obligations and vice versa. Such organizations suffered badly for growth and sustainability.

- **Stability vs. Change:** these two are critical elements of organizational success. While stability fosters continuity, efficiency, and security, change is essential for growth and sustainability in dynamic market environment. Managers require a nuanced approach to balance stability with the imperative of continuous change and adaptability. With rapid changes in market dynamics, technology, AI, etc. organization stability is often get disrupted now a days resulting frequent change in strategies and operations to sustain competitive position in the market. As the saying goes "change is constant" which is more common in managing organizational stability in changing circumstances. Management should remain alert and agile in manging changing landscape to achieve sustainable growth and results.

While the above paradoxes are quite apparent in any organization, question is how they should be managed? Best approach is to prepare the organization to manage these apparent paradoxes as a part of dynamic process of managerial adaptability embracing paradoxical and critical thinking by recognising and accepting the existence of contradictory demands.

It is therefore doubtful, if urging employees to put in more hours at the workplace will provide that kind of impetus for business growth. Managers should explore how to integrate and balance competing elements for greater good of the organization through creative thinking.

It is to be appreciated that decisions and strategies are not fixed but need to be continuously adjusted based on changing environment dynamics. Effective leadership is crucial in managing paradoxes through emotional intelligence, strategic foresight, and ability to communicate and align conflicting goals in a coherent manner.

Management paradoxes are not simply obstacles to be overcome but essential elements that define the complexity of modern organizations. The ability to embrace these contradictions and manage them effectively is a skill that distinguishes successful managers and organization from their counterparts. Rather than viewing paradoxes as a challenge to be solved they should be understood as opportunities for growth, creativity, and long term strategic advantage. As organizations continue to navigate an increasing volatile, uncertain, complex, and ambiguous world, the skilful handling of management paradoxes will likely become even more critical to organizational success. Empowering employees to take ownership of their roles and contribute to decision making foster a sense of purpose and enhances organizational performance.

In author's view, more particularly in an era of AI, this transformational change cannot be achieved by overworked employees and autocratic work culture which would be a sure cause of business failures.

10.
POLITICS AT WORK PLACE AND CONFLICT MANAGEMENT

Office politics and resultant conflict are quite common in corporate behaviour while jostling for promotions and career growth by employees. This appears to be more intense in an organization with limited growth opportunities for individuals to fulfil career ambitions. Each including seniors tend to behave in a conflicting manner to protect his or her position and turf at the cost of organizational performance, efficiency, productivity, and effectiveness. Office politics is also get influenced by likes and dislikes, biases, and prejudices of individual or a group. In such an atmosphere, dynamics of power, influence, and relationships can affect decision making, collaboration, and overall organizational culture. Workplace politics can create tension, reduce productivity, and lead to conflict. It makes and breaks many promising careers and causes individual hardships. Through office politics many get sadistic pleasures in undermining quality and talent of otherwise deserving individuals.

In some companies, the promoters who also manage the business, tend to be authoritative and want operations to be run as per their diktat. The plans keep changing frequently without accountability of such owner managers and invariably lower level managers are made scapegoats. In such an environment, how does an employee stand up to the owners and hold ground? Does the situation calls for HR training for owner managers? Ego centric and aggressive behaviour of owner managers often lead to blame game among departments, manpower attrition and may lead to lower revenue and profitability resulting gradual decline of the organization.

Office politics create an atmosphere where employees might spend more time engaging in political manoeuvres, gossips or conflict, it reduces productivity. Office politics creates favouritism, power struggles, and lack of transparency leading to low morale, dissatisfaction and stressful situations. Generally office politics leads to operating silos making collaboration difficult which impact teamwork. In such a situation employees may feel neglected, undervalued if promotions or rewards are based on political manoeuvring with bosses rather than merit based.

Author had experienced confrontations from colleagues and some seniors during his professional engagements in various capacities. More particularly, during phase of office promotions there were crab mentality to pull one down with disinformation, character assassination and other negative insinuation by many competing colleagues. Such politicking and behavioural pattern are more prevalent in PSUs work culture as many try to take advantages of their closeness to political bosses. Author remembers a situation when he was poised in a competitive position for a board level engagement. Prior to that, he was placed in a position with work responsibilities that would prevent him from any interactions with ministry officials by his senior to spoil his chances for career advancement.

In private sector, more particularly in family owned businesses, at senior positions, promoters' likes and dislikes based on biases, prejudices, and expectations of sycophancy often spoils growth opportunities to otherwise deserving professionals. Author had the privilege of being engaged in two family owned corporates, one global with local presence while other one is predominantly local. Author had observed without making any value judgement that a common thread seems to run in promoters' behavioural pattern though Global Group's approach was more sophisticated and subtle while that of local Company appeared more brazen. Over a period each group have cultivated a band of loyal and trusted sycophants who are generally available at their beck and call for doing all kind of dealings and are regarded as close confidants as part of extended family. Their opinions matter even in selection of outsiders. It is difficult for any professional with pride and ethical values to penetrate such coterie which often acts as informants and barriers. It is difficult for any upright professional to achieve that kind of trust and loyalty without bending and compromising ethical values.

There are, however, some positive side effects on office politics. Some may find it useful way for career advancement in engaging in office politics. Political savvy persons may find it easier, besides fast-track promotions, to secure resources or support for their projects with favourable decisions boosting performance in some areas.

While healthy transparent politics promote collaboration and success, toxic politics undermine both individual and team achievements. Unfortunately, office politics more often than not played out for individual gain rather than for the organizational benefits.

In order to mitigate the negative consequences of office politics, organization should encourage open communication to build up trust in the system to express concerns, grievances without fear of reprisal. HR policies should align in setting clear expectations and boundaries with monitoring, and periodic review based on honesty and transparency. Organization should align policies to promote respect, empathy, and accountability and are enforced consistently to foster inclusivity, collaboration and team work. Seniors should demonstrate transparency, ethical behaviour, fairness with integrity. However, such transparent and open system is not easy in family owned organizations due to deep rooted behavioural approach and attitudes while dealing with employees.

Organizational culture should evolve to equip employees with tools and training for managing interpersonal conflicts constructively. Organization should promote merit based recognitions based on performance and value addition instead of favouritism and office politics. Encourage employees to build emotional intelligence (EI) skills to understand, manage, and navigate social interactions more effectively. Clearly defined roles, responsibilities, and performance expectations will create favourable environment to minimise confusion and competition among employees through office politics.

11.
RANDOM THOUGHTS

In conclusion of this monograph, I thought of sharing my limited understanding of contemporary situations which is likely to impact entire mankind in some way or other. I must admit that I am not an economist or an IT specialist, nor so much knowledgeable about geopolitics. Views are purely based on being alive to newspaper readings, news channels, and some social media discourse.

Now a days, eminent thinkers are articulating their views on positive and negative impacts of artificial intelligence (AI) and how it is going to impact on employments and other aspects of human lives. It is being professed that with growing advent of AI, many white colour jobs in many professions would be redundant accelerating the scale of unemployment globally. Similarly use of robotics in manufacturing sector will reduce need of blue collar employees as well. Under such a situation how many countries are going to sustain growth momentum and wellbeing of citizens?

Let us look at our own country i.e. India. We are still a developing nation and one of the fasted growing nations globally in terms of GDP. We are the 4th largest economy at present and poised to become 3rd largest economy in a few years. However India is far behind top two economies viz. US

& China China's growth in past few decades is phenomenal. Around 1978 economies of both India and China were comparable. In fact, on certain parameters India was ahead. Since then China changed its strategy from rigid communist philosophy and embraced market economy in parallel opening many sectors for foreign investments and manufacturing hubs from multinational companies despite communist regime, single party rule, legal and financial systems not aligned with global practices. China since then has leapfrogged in capacity building, manufacturing, science and technology, space technology, defence, R&D, patents, infrastructure, rre earth components, etc. and it's GDP grew at 9-10% over the past several years though growth has petered off in recent years, but still growing albeit slowly. During this period, China not only created critical mass in many vital sectors including rare earth components, missile technology, nuclear energy, military hardwires, space technology, electronic chips, etc. During this phase it could able to contain its population through state regulation which is turning out to be counterproductive in recent times with growth of ageing population. Over a period it has become a global supply house in many commodities and has established quite a few global brands. China's scale of urban development with modern facilities, express ways, bullet trains, modern ports, etc. have surpassed many developed nations. China could able to achieve that kind of growth and world dominance in many exportable goods through determination, tenacity, planned and focussed approach. China's investment in R&D for automated systems and processes is significantly higher and comparable to many developed nations .

In comparison, India is far behind in all those aspects barring IT services though our GDP growth in recent years is higher than that of China. Our investment in R&D is also much smaller in comparison to other progressive nations. We have a dubious distinction of being most populous country in the world overtaking China in recent times. Compared to China our landmass is less and hence density of populations in most of urban, semi urban, and rural areas is very high and lacks many basic infrastructures like houses, health, education, quality roads, electricity, water supply, job oriented infrastructure growth, etc. compared to many other developing nations. We are also surrounded by hostile neighbouring countries requiring significant investments in defence sector. Our multi-party political structure and governance systems are not conducive for rapid growth. We are still preserving colonial mind set with obsolete rules and regulations. Many local parties follow vote bank politics and are oblivious to inherent dangers which creates obstacles for accelerated growth failing to harness talent pools, and potential, and hidden strengths of the country.

Though significant improvements have taken place in recent years due to present government's planned and focussed approach, problems remain. We are also burdened with large unemployment and under employment among unskilled, semiskilled, skilled, and educated youths particularly in semi urban and rural areas. India is considered to be a youthful nation with large segment of population falling under working level young category which is available for productive engagements. While it's a boon, it also remains a big challenge for the nation to harness the talent and potential of such vast majority of young aspirational populace. A large cross section of people are engaged in farming, manual and semiskilled activities in constructions, real estate, small scale industries, roadside repair & maintenance, etc. mostly in unorganised sectors in unhygienic conditions often lacking basic sustainability like income which remains low, accommodation, healthcare, education, etc. In search of employment a vast majority becomes migratory moving from place to place mostly concentrating in major cities where developments are happening in the form of construction of roads, real estates, hospitals, manufacturing, IT Hub, etc. causing congestion and strains on existing local infrastructure. It is also increasing pollution and unhygienic living conditions with the influx of more people in the cities. To improve the situation, metros, and urban areas are undertaking more development in already overstretched areas, bringing more labour from rural areas in search of jobs accentuating problems further. It is becoming a vicious circle due to unplanned growth. We hear almost daily plights of metro cities with broken roads, traffic congestion, clogged drainage systems, crumbling infrastructure, garbage, pollution, water accumulation during rainy seasons, etc. causing health hazards, and more distress to locals. To prevent such migration Governments is trying to develop other urban centres with facilities in various states, but the process is slow and cumbersome.

With economic growth, more and more youths are looking for employment preferably in government for continuity and sustainable lifestyle. Our media including social media are full of advertisements promoting high end products and services with the face of iconic and successful high net worth persona from film industry, sports, and other sought after fields. Such blatant projections is heightening the aspirations and desires of many, mostly from poor and middle class who can ill afford such goodies with their low level of income. Urge and desires for better lifestyles often culminates into unsocial and criminal activities which seem to be growing in our societies. With economic growth disparities of have and have-nots are also increasing causing social disturbances.

To meet growing needs of gainful employment of vast majority, government is trying its best to encourage small, medium, large industries, and start-ups, or expand existing businesses with inducements and policy changes. Govt. is also increasing its investments in various capital intensive projects to sustain growth and generate more employment. With emphasis on education, health, housing, sanitation, etc. and to cater to growing needs for higher education, more academic, technical, and medical institutions are being set up in different states. These initiatives are increasing number of educated youths year after year clamouring for sustainable employment which is becoming a Hobson's choice and a limiting factor, leading to growing anger and frustration among Gen Z.

Against this background, let us look into other aspects. To sustain economic growth and security, we need resources including foreign exchange and high end technologies most of which are still to be imported at least for the time being till country becomes self-sufficient in many of needed fields. In order to generate foreign exchange we have to export goods and services which are to be of world class to meet global competitions in terms of quality and price. For this our manufacturing, support systems, and supply chains have to be efficient, productive and cost competitive compared to other global suppliers. For this, our manufacturing ecosystems have to be not only robust, but productive and cost efficient with the support of automation, robotics, and use of emerging AI tools all requiring less manpower for manual intervention unless needed. This creates a conundrum. While more people are looking for jobs, manufacturing facilities are reducing hiring to remain globally competitive using modern automated technologies and processes. Global demand – supply depends on consumption behaviour particularly that of the developed countries. Due to various geopolitical reasons with latest trend of local market protection, the total size of the market is not increasing, in fact it is contracting. As a result there is intense competition among exporting nations to increase their market size. Countries having cutting edge technologies with high quality and innovative products and services at an affordable price are gaining advantage causing market disruptions in many ways.

In such a dynamic and ever changing market environment, India cannot afford to lag behind to protect its overseas market opportunities. Local industries not only have to play the game the way other competitors are playing but also to remain ahead to gain market advantages. This efforts are contracting in nature from the perspective of generating employment. It is a big challenge domestically for local industries and government to support ever enlarging pool of employable manpower unless business expands and/or new projects and more entrepreneurial opportunities emerge. Fortunately, unlike many other developing countries, India's domestic market is large. With the growth of semi urban and rural markets the pie size is increasing for consumable goods and services. Thus there is a large untapped markets yet to be exploited based on bottom of the pyramid principles as propounded by management guru Dr. C. K. Prahlad. This offers big opportunities to existing and new start-ups with innovative products and services. With the emphasis on 'Atmanirvar Bharat' by the government, digital economy, and encouragement to MSME in various business verticals, besides large industries, there is growth in employments. Despite all such initiatives, fresh employment generation is not keeping pace with the ever increasing number of employable and educated aspiring youths. Unfortunately, situation is getting compounded due to large-scale influx of people, mostly illegal, from neighbouring countries, resulting demographic shift in many states worsening the employment scenario besides socio-political disturbances.

AI is now posing different kind of challenges and disruptions globally. Regulatory framework being planned by various countries and timeframe are not keeping pace with AI development and its impact on societal ecosystem. Many industries globally have started reducing manpower partly due to contrarian demand pattern resulting from current geopolitics and economic scenario and partly due to adoption of AI tools.

While AI is raising industry level productivity and creating new business models and opportunities, as of now only a few high profile organizations could able to capture value. With its uses there is likelihood of upside in GDP but benefits will be uneven across countries and sectors as projected by economists. We are also observing job disruptions in many industries with demand for different skills and substantial reskilling needs. It is predicted that generative AI can automate routine tasks, enhance knowledge work, and speed up R&D efforts in many areas. While some early movers with integrated AI applications are benefiting with shorten product development cycle, automated customer support systems and reduced costs capturing higher value, many however may not see immediate gains. There are risks during initial phases leading to operational, service, business risks, supply chain disruptions and additional compliance costs requiring more management time and attention to mitigate such risks to derive higher value.

AI may increase tradable services, change comparative advantages, and reshape value chain. Countries, companies, having data, cloud, and skilled labour will benefit more.

There is however apprehension, which is not unfounded, about job losses with AI, studies show that many activities within jobs can be automated – but only a small share of occupations are fully automatable. It is very likely that many roles would be reshaped, not eliminated, requiring task reallocation new complimentary skills involving critical thinking and domain expertise. Demand for AI literate managers, data engineers, and others with required AI related skill base will grow with more and more adoption of AI by industries and businesses. Areas like health, education, supply chain, R&D, defence, manufacturing, retail, IT services, etc. will emerge front runners for AI applications. Unless properly regulated and managed, business disruptions due to cyber-attacks, spread of misinformation in social media, erosion of privacy, and job disruptions are likely negative consequences. In fact, we are already observing negative connotation of AI on various fronts with AI induced fake information using the face, images, and voice of well-known personalities in various social media channels. Unless we are watchful and Govt. takes timely corrective and regulatory measures, negative consequences in the society are going to be severe.

From above brief perspective, India is going to face several challenges and disruptions in many fronts unless planned wisely. Shape of outcomes will be determined as much by business strategy, workforce investment, skill development, public policy, governance processes, as well by the technology itself. From my perspective, in the medium to long run we are likely to see more AI enabled business opportunities due to availability of large pool of knowledgeable and talented youngsters, vast domestic markets, growth in incomes , exports, etc. which will generate employable opportunities for skilled manpower. Simultaneously, Government has to take bold measures and initiatives to curb infiltration of people from neighbouring countries, secure borders to prevent infiltrations, deport illegal immigrants who in many cases are taking away jobs of locals and are compounding negatively the economic situation which will cause more social and political disorder. Thus tasks ahead are challenging against various odds both domestically and externally with disruptive toolkits.

In summary, we shall see both growth and disruptions in our day to day life in AI era.

****

Some inferences in articles are drawn from following Authors and Management Gurus.

1. Ronald A. Heifez and Donald L. Lawrie.
2. Warren J. Bennis and Robert J. Thomas.
3. Jim Collins.
4. James Martin.
5. Haskett, Emeritus Professor of Harvard Business School.
6. John P. Kotter.
7. Built to Last by James C. Collins and Jerry I. Porras.
8. Dr. C. K. Prahlad.

ABOUT THE AUTHOR

Dr. Indra Nath Chatterjee hails from a middle class family at Chandannagar, West Bengal. He had his schooling and college education from his home town and later did his Management from Indian Institute of Management, Calcutta. He also acquired other professional qualifications like FCS, FCMA and some others while working. He pursued Advance Courses from University of Texas, Dallas and from Kellogg Graduate School of Management, Chicago, USA. Later, he did his Ph. D. in Management from Symbiosis International University, Pune. Dr. Chatterjee was associated with a number of reputed organizations, both PSU & Private companies at various senior executive levels including board levels. During his prolonged service and professional career, he had to travel widely within and outside the country. Dr. Chatterjee and his wife Pahari reside in Mumbai at present while their only son Ujjal lives abroad with his wife Tulika and son Avighna.

